Revising U.S. Grand Strategy Toward China

COUNCIL *on*
FOREIGN
RELATIONS

Council Special Report No. 72
March 2015

Robert D. Blackwill and Ashley J. Tellis

Revising U.S. Grand Strategy Toward China

The Council on Foreign Relations (CFR) is an independent, nonpartisan membership organization, think tank, and publisher dedicated to being a resource for its members, government officials, business executives, journalists, educators and students, civic and religious leaders, and other interested citizens in order to help them better understand the world and the foreign policy choices facing the United States and other countries. Founded in 1921, CFR carries out its mission by maintaining a diverse membership, with special programs to promote interest and develop expertise in the next generation of foreign policy leaders; convening meetings at its headquarters in New York and in Washington, DC, and other cities where senior government officials, members of Congress, global leaders, and prominent thinkers come together with Council members to discuss and debate major international issues; supporting a Studies Program that fosters independent research, enabling CFR scholars to produce articles, reports, and books and hold roundtables that analyze foreign policy issues and make concrete policy recommendations; publishing *Foreign Affairs*, the preeminent journal on international affairs and U.S. foreign policy; sponsoring Independent Task Forces that produce reports with both findings and policy prescriptions on the most important foreign policy topics; and providing up-to-date information and analysis about world events and American foreign policy on its website, CFR.org.

The Council on Foreign Relations takes no institutional positions on policy issues and has no affiliation with the U.S. government. All views expressed in its publications and on its website are the sole responsibility of the author or authors.

Council Special Reports (CSRs) are concise policy briefs, produced to provide a rapid response to a developing crisis or contribute to the public's understanding of current policy dilemmas. CSRs are written by individual authors—who may be CFR fellows or acknowledged experts from outside the institution—in consultation with an advisory committee, and are intended to take sixty days from inception to publication. The committee serves as a sounding board and provides feedback on a draft report. It usually meets twice— once before a draft is written and once again when there is a draft for review; however, advisory committee members, unlike Task Force members, are not asked to sign off on the report or to otherwise endorse it. Once published, CSRs are posted on www.cfr.org.

For further information about CFR or this Special Report, please write to the Council on Foreign Relations, 58 East 68th Street, New York, NY 10065, or call the Communications office at 212.434.9888. Visit our website, CFR.org.

To submit a letter in response to a Council Special Report for publication on our website, CFR.org, you may send an email to CSReditor@cfr.org. Alternatively, letters may be mailed to us at: Publications Department, Council on Foreign Relations, 58 East 68th Street, New York, NY 10065. Letters should include the writer's name, postal address, and daytime phone number. Letters may be edited for length and clarity, and may be published online. Please do not send attachments. All letters become the property of the Council on Foreign Relations and will not be returned. We regret that, owing to the volume of correspondence, we cannot respond to every letter.

Contents

Foreword

It has become something of a cliché to say that no relationship will matter more when it comes to defining the twenty-first century than the one between the United States and China. Like many clichés, this statement is true but not terribly useful, as it tells us little or nothing about the nature of the relationship in question.

Some point to history and argue that strategic rivalry is highly likely if not inevitable between the existing major power of the day and the principal rising power. Others challenge such a prediction, emphasizing more the impact of domestic political, economic, and social developments within the two countries as well as the potential constructive influence of diplomacy and statecraft.

Robert D. Blackwill and Ashley J. Tellis, the authors of this Council Special Report, reach a conclusion considerably closer to the first of these two propositions. "China represents and will remain the most significant competitor to the United States for decades to come," they write, judging that "the likelihood of a long-term strategic rivalry between Beijing and Washington is high." They also argue that China has not evolved into the "responsible stakeholder" that many in the United States hoped it would. To the contrary, Blackwill and Tellis see China as having adopted a grand strategy for itself that is meant to increase state control over Chinese society and, beyond its borders, to pacify its periphery, cement its status in the international system, and replace the United States as the most important power in Asia.

What flows from this assessment is nothing less than a call on their part for "a new grand strategy toward China that centers on balancing the rise of Chinese power rather than continuing to assist its ascendancy." The two authors acknowledge that this new policy "cannot be built on a bedrock of containment"; they also say that policymakers cannot simply jettison the prevailing policy of integration. But they do advocate what they describe as "crucial changes to the current policy in order to limit the dangers that China's economic and military expansion pose to U.S. interests in Asia and globally."

Stated somewhat differently, the authors recommend a new U.S. policy of balancing China that would in effect change the balance of current U.S. policy, in the process placing less emphasis on support and cooperation and more on pressure and competition. There would be less hedging and more active countering.

A number of policy prescriptions follow, including the adoption of policies designed to produce more robust economic growth in the United States; new trade arrangements in Asia that exclude China; a stricter technology-control regime affecting exports to China; a larger, more capable, and more active U.S. air and naval presence in the Asia-Pacific region; more intimate U.S. strategic ties with Japan, Australia, the Republic of Korea, India, the countries of southeast Asia, and Taiwan; and a considerably tougher set of measures to counter Chinese behavior in the cyber realm.

Interestingly, the report also argues for an intensification of U.S.-Chinese diplomatic contacts, recommending a discourse that is "more candid, high-level, and private than current practice." The focus of such talks would be not on the internal political character of China, but on such issues as Asian security, and would possibly involve experienced external persons on both sides who would presumably be less constrained by the sorts of rigidities and conventional thinking normally associated with bureaucracies.

It is clear, though, that this call for real dialogue is not motivated by any great optimism of what it can achieve. Indeed, the authors conclude by noting that "the most that can be hoped for is caution and restrained predictability by the two sides as intense U.S.-China strategic competition becomes the new normal, and even that will be no easy task to achieve in the period ahead."

Both authors anticipate that their analysis and recommendations alike will be controversial and generate substantial criticism, and they devote their conclusion to addressing what they see as the likely challenges to what they have written. I expect some readers will, as a result, be persuaded by what is said here; I equally expect that others will remain unpersuaded that what is being suggested in these pages is either desirable or feasible. But whatever the reaction or reactions, *Revising*

U.S. Grand Strategy Toward China deserves to become an important part of the debate about U.S. foreign policy and the pivotal U.S.-China relationship.

Richard N. Haass
President
Council on Foreign Relations
March 2015

Acknowledgments

We would like to express our gratitude to the many people who made this report possible. To begin, we thank CFR President Richard N. Haass and Director of Studies James M. Lindsay for their support of this project and insightful feedback throughout the drafting process.

We owe a debt to the members of the CFR study group on U.S. grand strategy toward China for their comments and critiques, all of which improved the substance of the report. The report also benefited from interviews conducted with current and former U.S. government officials, as well as insights from researchers and journalists immersed in the U.S.-China relationship.

We are grateful for the valuable assistance of Patricia Dorff, Eli Dvorkin, and Ashley Bregman in CFR's Publications Department, who provided editorial support, and to Melinda Wuellner and Kendra Davidson in Global Communications and Media Relations for their marketing efforts. We also appreciate the contributions of the David Rockefeller Studies Program staff in shepherding the report. Most important, we thank Research Associate Lauren Dickey, our gifted CFR sinologist, whose contribution to this report was indispensable. Special thanks also goes to William Hayes of the Carnegie Endowment for International Peace for his editorial and research assistance.

This publication was made possible through support from the Robina Foundation. The statements made and views expressed herein are solely our own.

Robert D. Blackwill
Ashley J. Tellis

Acronyms

APEC	Asia-Pacific Economic Community
ASEAN	Association of Southeast Asian Nations
BMD	ballistic missile defense
CCP	Chinese Communist Party
IMET	International Military Exchange Training
IMF	International Monetary Fund
OECD	Organization for Economic Cooperation and Development
PAP	People's Armed Police
PLA	People's Liberation Army
PRC	People's Republic of China
ROK	Republic of Korea
TPP	Trans-Pacific Partnership
TRA	Taiwan Relations Act
UNSC	United Nations Security Council
WTO	World Trade Organization

Council Special Report

Introduction

In a classic work published at the height of the Second World War, *Makers of Modern Strategy: Military Thought from Machiavelli to Hitler*, editor Edward Meade Earle defined grand strategy as "the art of controlling and utilizing the resources of a nation…to the end that its vital interests shall be effectively promoted and secured against enemies, actual, potential, or merely presumed."[1] Elaborating on this idea, Earle argued that this "highest type of strategy" is precisely such because it "so integrates the policies and armaments of the nation that the resort to war is either rendered unnecessary or is undertaken with the maximum chance of victory."[2] With these considerations in mind, Earle correctly concluded that "[grand] strategy…is not merely a concept of wartime, but is an inherent element of statecraft at all times."[3] Though many others have subsequently offered variations on this concept, a wiser or more comprehensive definition of grand strategy has not been better articulated.

Since its founding, the United States has consistently pursued a grand strategy focused on acquiring and maintaining preeminent power over various rivals, first on the North American continent, then in the Western hemisphere, and finally globally. During the Cold War, this strategy was manifested in the form of "containment," which provided a unifying vision of how the United States could protect its systemic primacy as well as its security, ensure the safety of its allies, and eventually enable the defeat of its adversary, the Soviet Union. As Melvyn P. Leffler succinctly summarized, "the key goals of containment were to limit the spread of Soviet power and communist ideology. Yet containment was never a defensive strategy; it was conceived as an instrument to achieve victory in the Cold War."[4] A variety of policies—including deliberately limiting Soviet connectivity with the major global economic centers of power, sustaining a diverse and sometimes overlapping set of "mutual security agreements" and formal alliances, pursuing worldwide ideological campaigns to delegitimize the Soviet state and its policies, and preserving the United States' industrial and technological supremacy—were successfully implemented to achieve this aim as Washington entered a new era of geopolitical competition.

In the aftermath of the American victory in the Cold War and the dissolution of containment, U.S. policymakers have struggled to conceptualize a grand strategy that would prove adequate to the nation's new circumstances beyond the generic desire to protect the liberal international order underwritten by American power in the postwar era. Though the Department of Defense during the George H.W. Bush administration presciently contended that its "strategy must now refocus on precluding the emergence of any potential future global competitor"—thereby consciously pursuing the strategy of primacy that the United States successfully employed to outlast the Soviet Union—there was some doubt at the time whether that document reflected Bush 41 policy.[5] In any case, no administration in Washington has either consciously or consistently pursued such an approach. To the contrary, a series of administrations have continued to implement policies that have actually enabled the rise of new competitors, such as China, despite the fact that the original impulse for these policies—the successful containment of the Soviet Union—lost their justification with the demise of Soviet power.

Because the American effort to "integrate" China into the liberal international order has now generated new threats to U.S. primacy in Asia—and could eventually result in a consequential challenge to American power globally—Washington needs a new grand strategy toward China that centers on balancing the rise of Chinese power rather than continuing to assist its ascendancy. This strategy cannot be built on a bedrock of containment, as the earlier effort to limit Soviet power was, because of the current realities of globalization. Nor can it involve simply jettisoning the prevailing policy of integration. Rather, it must involve crucial changes to the current policy in order to limit the dangers that China's economic and military expansion pose to U.S. interests in Asia and globally.

These changes, which constitute the heart of an alternative balancing strategy, must derive from the clear recognition that preserving U.S. primacy in the global system ought to remain the central objective of U.S. grand strategy in the twenty-first century. Sustaining this status in the face of rising Chinese power requires, among other things, revitalizing the U.S. economy to nurture those disruptive innovations that bestow on the United States asymmetric economic advantages over others; creating new preferential trading arrangements among U.S. friends and allies to increase their mutual gains through instruments that consciously exclude China; recreating a technology-control regime involving U.S. allies that prevents China from acquiring military and strategic capabilities enabling it to inflict "high-leverage strategic harm" on the United States and its partners; concertedly building up the power-political capacities of U.S. friends and allies on China's periphery; and improving the capability of U.S. military forces to effectively project power along the Asian rimlands despite any Chinese opposition—all while continuing to work with China in the diverse ways that befit its importance to U.S. national interests.

The necessity for such a balancing strategy that deliberately incorporates elements that limit China's capacity to misuse its growing power, even as the United States and its allies continue to interact with China diplomatically and economically, is driven by the likelihood that a long-term strategic rivalry between Beijing and Washington is high. China's sustained economic success over the past thirty-odd years has enabled it to aggregate formidable power, making it the nation most capable of dominating the Asian continent and thus undermining the traditional U.S. geopolitical objective of ensuring that this arena remains free of hegemonic control. The meteoric growth of the Chinese economy, even as China's per capita income remains behind that of the United States in the near future, has already provided Beijing with the resources necessary to challenge the security of both its Asian neighbors and Washington's influence in Asia, with dangerous consequences. Even as China's overall gross domestic product (GDP) growth slows considerably in the future, its relative growth rates are likely to be higher than those of the United States for the foreseeable future, thus making the need to balance its rising power important. Only a fundamental collapse of the Chinese state would free Washington from the obligation of systematically balancing Beijing, because even the alternative of a modest Chinese stumble would not eliminate the dangers presented to the United States in Asia and beyond.

Of all nations—and in most conceivable scenarios—China is and will remain the most significant competitor to the United States for decades to come.[6] China's rise thus far has already bred geopolitical, military, economic, and ideological challenges to U.S. power, U.S.

allies, and the U.S.-dominated international order. Its continued, even if uneven, success in the future would further undermine U.S. national interests. Washington's current approach toward Beijing, one that values China's economic and political integration in the liberal international order at the expense of the United States' global preeminence and long-term strategic interests, hardly amounts to a "grand" strategy, much less an effective one. The need for a more coherent U.S. response to increasing Chinese power is long overdue.

China's Evolving Grand Strategy

Following the Communist Revolution in 1949, China has pursued the objective of maximizing its national power in order to recover the geopolitical primacy it enjoyed in East Asia prior to the Columbian era. The arrival of modernity proved unkind to China's regional predominance—and, in an economic sense, its global standing—embittering its Maoist founders, who were determined, through their communist uprising, to retrieve the greatness last witnessed during the mid-Qing Dynasty, which had been lost due to technological atrophy, domestic conflict, and external intervention.

Given this painful history, it is not surprising that China's primary strategic goal in contemporary times has been the accumulation of "comprehensive national power."[7] This pursuit of power in all its dimensions—economic, military, technological, and diplomatic—is driven by the conviction that China, a great civilization undone by the hostility of others, could never attain its destiny unless it amassed the power necessary to ward off the hostility of those opposed to this quest. This conception, shared by all Chinese leaders since 1949, reflects a vision of politics that views conflict as intrinsic to the human condition. In this "parabellum paradigm," superior power alone creates order. China's success as a state requires its leaders to possess greater capabilities than any other entity inside or outside its borders.[8]

The failure to create such a hierarchy centered on the conjoint supremacy of the Chinese Communist Party (CCP) within the country and China's primacy within the international system would open the door to persistent and dangerous threats of the kind witnessed during China's "century of national humiliation."[9] Defeating these dangers requires that the party protect its monopoly over power within the country while steadily acquiring more power than its international competitors. As Chinese theorist Ye Zicheng argues in his treatise on Chinese grand strategy, "There is a close connection between the rejuvenation of the Chinese nation and China's becoming a world power. If China does not become a world power, the rejuvenation of the Chinese nation will be incomplete. Only when it becomes a world power can we say that the total rejuvenation of the Chinese nation has been achieved."[10]

This vision of strengthening the Chinese state while recovering China's centrality in international politics—both objectives requiring the accumulation of "comprehensive national power"—suggests that the aims of Beijing's grand strategy both implicate and transcend the United States' and China's other Asian rivals. For China, which is simultaneously an ancient civilization and a modern polity, grand strategic objectives are not simply about desirable rank orderings in international politics but rather about fundamental conceptions of order.[11]

Good order in the Chinese world view is ensured by the creation of a durable hierarchy: an absolute, virtuous sovereign on the inside and geopolitical primacy on the outside. However, the "rejuvenation of the Chinese nation" involves more than its strengthening as a state and its rise to the pinnacle of the international hierarchy. More fundamentally, it requires that others accept this order as legitimate, which the historian Wang Gungwu has described as a "principle of superiority" underwriting Beijing's "long-hallowed tradition of treating foreign countries as all alike but unequal and inferior to China."[12] Consistent with this principle, Henry Kissinger, describing the traditional sinocentric system, has correctly noted that China "considered itself, in a sense, the sole sovereign government of the world," wherein the emperor's purview was not "a sovereign state of 'China'…but 'All Under Heaven,' of which China formed the central, civilized part."[13]

Because the acquisition of comprehensive national power is therefore meant to both increase the Chinese state's control over its society and maximize the country's overall capabilities relative to its foreign competitors, Beijing has consistently pursued four specific operational aims since the revolution—though the instruments used to achieve these ends have varied over time.

MAINTAIN INTERNAL ORDER

The first and most important aim pursued by China's leaders since the founding of the modern Chinese state has been the preservation of internal order. Though this resolute pursuit of internal order was rooted in the CCP's self-interest, it also stemmed from a deeper Chinese phobia "of social chaos and political fragmentation or collapse, usually seen as 'just-around-the-corner' and often closely associated with [fears of] aggression and intervention from the outside."[14] Because of the historical memory of domestic divisions providing incentives for foreign manipulation and even aggression, China's rulers have sought to suppress all political disquiet—increasingly by appeals to nationalism, but by coercion when necessary.

In contemporary times, this fixation on preserving domestic order has become particularly acute, paradoxically because of China's recent economic success. High growth has resulted in desires for expanded personal liberties, but the regime has responded by restricting freedom of expression in various realms. Rapid economic growth has also dramatically accentuated stratification and social inequalities while increasing social dislocation and corruption nationally. As a result, the same tool that has accelerated China's rise in the global system has also weakened the CCP's domestic legitimacy, and political resentment against Beijing has grown, especially in the Han-minority areas of the country.

Despite China's meteoric economic success, its leadership does not possess easy solutions to the current challenges of governance and legitimacy. Surrendering power in favor of genuine democracy is unthinkable for the Communist regime, and the palliatives offered by anticorruption campaigns, the incorporation of rule by law (as opposed to rule *of* law), the increased invocation of classical texts in an effort to seek validation in tradition, the growing ideological emphasis on promoting "Chinese values," the promotion of a new "Chinese Dream" centered on "national rejuvenation, improvement of people's livelihoods, prosperity, construction of a better society, and military strengthening," and the stimulation of nationalism have not yet resolved the crisis of legitimacy that now engulfs the CCP.[15]

China's Communist rulers remain threatened by U.S. campaigns in support of democracy, the rule of law, and the protection of minorities, all of which are viewed in Beijing as thinly veiled attempts at either fomenting secession or engineering regime change. In an effort to ensure that American democratic values and policies do not undermine the CCP's hold on power, Chinese rulers have prosecuted a multipronged ideological campaign that includes a strident defense of sovereignty and a concerted rejection of all foreign interest in the nation's internal affairs, intense surveillance of suspect domestic groups and nongovernmental organizations operating in China, and focused propaganda efforts to amplify Chinese nationalism and mobilize public support in defense of the regime and the state.[16]

Beneath these ideational efforts, however, lies the iron fist. Given the CCP's deep-seated fears for its own survival amid the current economic and social ferment in China, the party has continually expanded its capabilities for domestic coercion, to the point where its internal security budget, exemplified by the People's Armed Police (PAP), is larger than that of the People's Liberation Army (PLA) itself. Clearly, internal security competes with, and could even trump, external security. Further complicating matters, the party's army fears finding itself in the awkward position of having to defend the purported representatives of the people against the people's own wrath—a conundrum that may prove to be explosive if events like Tiananmen Square were to recur in the future.

SUSTAIN HIGH ECONOMIC GROWTH

Preserving internal control remains the foremost objective of the CCP today. But the goal of ensuring continued and unchallenged Communist rule leads to the second operational aspiration: sustaining the high levels of economic growth necessary to preserve social order. Since the founding of the Communist state, transforming the Chinese economy has remained an important political aim. After all, Mao Zedong had no doubts that political power grew out of not only a monopoly of force, but, more fundamentally, material foundations.

Unfortunately for China, however, Mao's collectivist strategies failed to achieve the high levels of growth chalked up by its neighbors, and his capricious political actions only further stunted China's development. Yet so long as Mao remained alive, his towering personality and his ruthless politics—especially the extreme and effective brutality of the PLA and the Red Guards—ensured that the CCP's hold on power did not suffer because of economic underperformance.[17]

Since the beginning of the reform period under Deng Xiaoping, however, high levels of economic growth have become *indispensable.* In the absence of charismatic leaders such as Mao and Deng, economic growth has become important for sustaining the legitimacy of the CCP—even for China's current "imperial president," Xi Jinping.[18]

With the shift to market reforms beginning in 1978, the imperative for high growth has only intensified as the distinctiveness of the CCP as the vanguard of socialism has progressively eroded. There is nothing particularly unique about the party anymore, except that it remains the sole holder of political power in China.

Why this should be the case in perpetuity remains difficult to answer—and the party has sought to deflect this question by, in effect, promising high levels of sustained economic growth as its newest justification for continued rule. This strategy of mitigating a fraying political legitimacy through impressive economic performance has come to embody the essence of the new social contract in China: through its economic policies, the party promises rising standards of living for China's population and an increase in personal (but not political) freedoms in exchange for an unchallenged acceptance of continued Communist rule. For the moment at least, this strategy appears to be successful. For whatever its discontent may be, the Chinese population ultimately ends up supporting the regime because it views order and control as essential for maintaining the high rates of economic growth that generate the prosperity demanded by the citizenry. The populace and the party are thus locked into an uncertain symbiosis that provides the regime with strength and the polity with a modicum of stability—a relationship that compels China's leaders to maintain strong economic ties with the outside world while protecting the country's claims and prerogatives internationally as the price of political success at home.

The aim of sustaining high levels of economic growth, therefore, is colored by both economic and political imperatives. The former speak to the development agenda of the Chinese state—the importance of lifting vast numbers of people out of poverty and enriching the population at the fastest rate possible—while the latter are advanced by the fact that rapid economic expansion contributes to the CCP's political legitimacy, increases its available resources for domestic and international (including military) ends, and underwrites its status and material claims in the international arena. China's means of producing high economic growth have also been distinctive. By liberalizing commodity and labor prices but not the prices of other elements such as land, capital, and energy, Beijing created limited free markets in China that operated under the supervision of a strong and controlling state. Because many foreign firms invested in China under this scheme, manufacturing consumer and industrial goods intended primarily for export, China has become the "new workshop of the world."[19]

This economic model of production for overseas markets is slowly changing: it is now supplemented by increasing attention to domestic consumers and by the rise of new private enterprises, but it was controlled capitalism that elevated China's growth to unprecedented levels, thus permitting Beijing to portray its older approach—which consisted of incremental reforms, innovation and experimentation, export-led growth, state-dominated capitalism, and authoritarian politics—as the superior alternative to the American framework of free markets overseen by democratic regimes. The global financial crisis of 2007–2008 raised doubts about the wisdom of Washington's methods of economic management, giving new life to China's critique of liberal democracy and free markets.

Although the attractiveness, endurance, and exportability of this so-called Beijing model are suspect on multiple grounds, the fact remains that it has more or less served China well until now.[20] This model has bequeathed Beijing with huge investible surpluses (in the form of vast foreign exchange reserves), substantially increased its technological capabilities (thanks to both legitimate and illegitimate acquisitions of proprietary knowledge), and—most important—has tied the wider global economy ever more tightly to China.

Although this last development has generated wealth and welfare gains globally, it has also produced several unnerving strategic consequences. It has made many of China's trading partners, especially its smaller neighbors, asymmetrically dependent on China and thus reluctant to voice opposition even when China's policies leave them disadvantaged.[21] China's economic integration has also produced higher relative gains for itself, even with its larger trading partners, such as the United States—not in the narrow sense pertaining to the bilateral terms of trade, but in the larger strategic sense that its overall growth has risen far faster than it might have had China remained locked into the autarkic policies of the pre-reform period. U.S. support for China's entry into the global trading system has thus created the awkward situation in which Washington has contributed toward hastening Beijing's economic growth and, by extension, accelerated its rise as a geopolitical rival. Furthermore, China's growing economic ties have nurtured and encouraged various internal constituencies within China's trading partners to pursue parochial interests that often diverge from their countries' larger national interests with regard to China.[22] Finally, economic integration has shaped the leadership perceptions of many of China's trading partners in ways that lead them to worry about their dependence on and vulnerability to China. Even if such worry is sometimes exaggerated, it weakens their resistance to both Chinese blandishments and coercion.[23] Given these outcomes, it should not be surprising that Beijing has consciously sought to use China's growing economic power in a choking embrace designed to prevent its Asian neighbors from challenging its geopolitical interests, including weakening the U.S. alliance system in Asia.

Beijing's commitment to sustaining high economic growth through deepened international interdependence, therefore, provides it not only with internal gains—a more pliant populace and a more powerful state—but consequential external benefits as well, in the form of a growing military and deferential neighbors who fear the economic losses that might arise from any political opposition to China. These gains are likely to persist even as China's economic growth slows down over time—as it inevitably will—so long as Beijing's overall material power and its relative growth rates remain superior to those of its neighbors.[24]

PACIFY THE PERIPHERY

The external advantages arising from China's high growth rates thus far have strengthened its capacity to achieve the third operational aim deriving from its quest for comprehensive national power: the pacification of its extended geographic periphery. With the success of economic reforms in the 1980s and 1990s, Beijing finally reacquired the means to pursue as an element of its grand strategy a systematic pacification of its extended peripheries and entrench Chinese dominance in the Indo-Pacific for decades to come.

The circumstances surrounding this renewed effort at pacification, however, were dramatically different from those of previous imperial eras. For one thing, China was now surrounded by major power competitors, such as Russia, Japan, and India. Furthermore, even the smaller states previously deferential to China at some point in the past, such as South Korea and Vietnam, were now successful, self-regarding entities that, despite their weaknesses, demonstrated no interest in being subservient to China. And, finally, the desire to sanitize the periphery to benefit Chinese supremacy in Asia now ran up against the ubiquitous presence of the United States, its forward-based and forward-operating military forces, and its formidable alliance system in Asia.

Facing this new environment, Beijing has advanced a variety of policies aimed toward pacifying its periphery. First, it has used its deep economic ties with its Asian neighbors to "reduce regional anxieties" about the rise of the People's Republic of China (PRC) while "creating mechanisms for Beijing to increase its influence with these regional neighbors."[25] Second, it has sought to make common cause with some states, such as Russia, which, despite their own suspicions of Beijing, have reasons—the Ukraine crisis and Western economic sanctions in the case of Moscow—to resist joining the larger balancing against China now under way in Asia.[26] Third, Beijing has embarked on a concerted modernization of the PLA with the intention to amass military power capable of both defeating local adversaries and deterring the United States from coming to their defense in a crisis.[27] Fourth, it has now renewed older efforts to delegitimize the U.S. alliance system in Asia, acting on its recognition that Washington remains the critical obstacle in Beijing's quest for a neutralized periphery. Accordingly, China has actively promoted "a new security concept" that rejects U.S. alliances as anachronisms; demands that Asian security be managed by Asians alone; and privileges China as the regional security provider of choice in a situation where, as Xi Jinping recently put it, "development is the greatest form of security."[28]

The desire to pacify the periphery thus signifies a modern adaption of the traditional aim to entrench China's centrality in Asia. If Beijing can successfully achieve these aims alongside a backdrop of continued internal stability, sustained economic growth, and expanding military capabilities, China's ambition to dominate Asia would over time recreate a bipolar system internationally. This achievement, in turn, would further reinforce the CCP's central domestic objective: delivering material benefits to the Chinese population while further increasing the country's security and standing, thereby assuring its continued grip on power.

CEMENT INTERNATIONAL STATUS

The CCP's desire to preserve domestic control is enhanced by the final element of the strategic goal of maximizing comprehensive national power: enhancing China's status as a central actor in the international system. Even before the Communist Revolution in 1949, China's prospects for becoming a major power were assured, as it was given a permanent, veto-wielding seat in the UN Security Council (UNSC). After President Richard Nixon and Secretary of State Henry Kissinger engineered the American rapprochement with Mao's China in 1971, China's role among the global elite—those few countries charged with managing the international order—was seamlessly transferred to the Communist regime in Beijing. Although such symbolic primacy seemed hollow when China underperformed economically, it was still critical in strategic terms insofar as it ensured that no fundamental decisions involving the UNSC could be made without China's consent.

Now that China has become a consequential economic power, its membership in the Security Council has only taken on additional significance—a fact highlighted by Beijing's determination to avoid any expansion of this body that could dilute its own longstanding privileges. Even beyond the Security Council, however, China's growing material capabilities have ensured that it becomes fundamentally relevant to all institutions of global order. Unsurprisingly, it has sought increasing power in these bodies—for example, in the International Monetary Fund (IMF) and the World Bank—to orient their operations toward serving its own purposes. Whether in the functional institutions or in regional ones, China has indeed "gone global," seeking and taking an active role to ensure that the rules made in these bodies not only do not undermine its interests, but also actively advance them.[29] In so doing, China's behaviors are similar to those of other previous rising powers in international politics.

China's widespread participation in international institutions today, nonetheless, has produced a mixed record. In some cases, China's activism has been beneficial for global order, but in many other instances Beijing has displayed an unwillingness to bear the commensurate costs of contributing toward global governance. Despite possessing the world's second-largest economy and military budget, China has generally adopted a strategy of burden shifting, insisting that the

United States and others bear the costs of providing global public goods even as China, citing its challenges as a "developing country," uses them to maximize its own national power. When international institutions are not perceived as advancing Chinese interests, the Chinese government has attempted to create or strengthen alternatives, especially ones that exclude the United States. For example, China has sought to integrate both its Brazil, Russia, India, China, and South Africa (BRICS) partners and its regional neighbors into economic ventures that rival those of the liberal international system, including the New Development Bank (widely perceived as an alternative to the World Bank and the IMF); the Regional Comprehensive Economic Partnership (RCEP), an Association of Southeast Asian Nations (ASEAN)–initiated free trade agreement (FTA) that China has ardently championed; an Asian Infrastructure Investment Bank (a rival to the Asian Development Bank); and an Asia-Pacific FTA (that would knit China closer to its neighbors in Asia). In other regions of the world, Beijing has initiated the Forum on China-Africa Cooperation, the China-Arab Cooperation Forum, and a variety of similar bodies that privilege China's position and undermine standards of governance set by the Organization for Economic Cooperation and Development (OECD), the World Bank, and other international institutions.

The character of Beijing's international involvement, therefore, suggests that its commitment to the current order is considerably instrumental. China is content to operate within that order to the degree that it receives material or status benefits, but it has no fundamental commitment to protecting that system beyond the gains incurred. At one level, this should not be surprising because, as Kissinger astutely noted, China is still "adjusting [itself] to membership in an international system designed in its absence on the basis of programs it did not participate in developing."[30] But, when all is considered, this ambivalence ultimately undermines American national interests and, most important, the premise on which the current U.S. strategy of integration is based: that China's entry into the liberal order will result over time in securing its support for that regime, to include the avoidance of threats levied against its principal guardian, the United States.[31]

Because these twin expectations have not materialized, China's rise as a new great power promises to be a troubling prospect for the United States for many years to come. China's economic growth derives considerably from its participation in the multilateral trading system and the larger liberal international order more generally, but its resulting military expansion has placed Beijing's economic strategy at odds with its political objective of threatening the guarantor of global interdependence, the United States. At the moment, China displays no urgency in addressing this conundrum, aware that its trading partners hesitate to pressure Beijing because of the potential for economic losses that might ensue. Given this calculation, Chinese leaders conclude that their country can continue to benefit from international trade without having to make any fundamental compromises in their existing disputes with other Asian states or their efforts to weaken U.S. power projection in Asia.

So long as the United States does not alter the intense "global code-pendency" that currently defines U.S.-China economic relations, China is content to maintain the current arrangement.[32] China still seeks to cooperate with the United States whenever possible, but only when such collaboration is not unduly burdensome in the face of common interests, does not undercut its geopolitical ambitions to undermine U.S. primacy, and does not foreclose future options that might one day prove advantageous to China. Because China recognizes that its quest for comprehensive national power is still incomplete, it seeks to avoid any confrontation with the United States or the international system in the near term. Rather, Beijing aims to deepen ties with all its global part-ners—and especially with Washington—in the hope that its accelerated rise and centrality to international trade and politics will compel others to become increasingly deferential to China's preferences. Should such obeisance not emerge once China has successfully risen, Beijing would then be properly equipped to protect its equities by force and at a lower cost than it could today, given that it is still relatively weak and remains reliant on the benefits of trade and global interdependence.

The fundamental conclusion for the United States, therefore, is that China does not see its interests served by becoming just another "trading state," no matter how constructive an outcome that might be for resolving the larger tensions between its economic and geopolitical strategies. Instead, China will continue along the path to becoming a conventional great power with the full panoply of political and military capabilities, all oriented toward realizing the goal of recovering from the United States the primacy it once enjoyed in Asia as a prelude to exerting global influence in the future.

U.S. Grand Strategy Toward China and U.S. Vital National Interests

The principal task that confronts U.S. grand strategy today, therefore, is adapting to the fundamental challenge posed by China's continuing rise. Integration, the prevailing U.S. approach toward China and the one followed assiduously since the 1970s, has undoubtedly contributed to China's rise as a future rival to American power. None of the alternatives usually discussed in the debates in Washington and elsewhere about how to respond to China's growing strength satisfy the objective of preserving American primacy for yet another "long cycle" in international politics. These alternatives, which include embracing and participating with China, accommodating Beijing through some kind of a Group of Two (G2) arrangement, or containing China à la the Soviet Union, all have severe limitations from the viewpoint of U.S. national interests and could in fact undermine the larger goal of strengthening Washington's preeminence in the global system.[33] Accordingly, the United States should substantially modify its grand strategy toward China—one that at its core would replace the goal of concentrating on integrating Beijing into the international system with that of consciously balancing its rise—as a means of protecting simultaneously the security of the United States and its allies, the U.S. position at the apex of the global hierarchy, and the strength of the liberal international order, which is owed ultimately to the robustness of American relative power.

There is no better basis for analyzing and formulating U.S. grand strategy toward China than connecting that strategy directly to U.S. vital national interests—conditions that are strictly necessary to safeguard and enhance Americans' survival and well-being in a free and secure nation.[34]

U.S. vital national interests are as follows:

- prevent, deter, and reduce the threat of conventional and unconventional attacks on the continental United States and its extended territorial possessions;

- maintain a balance of power in Europe and Asia that promotes peace and stability through a continuing U.S. leadership role and U.S. alliances;
- prevent the use and slow the spread of nuclear weapons and other weapons of mass destruction, secure nuclear weapons and materials, and prevent proliferation of intermediate and long-range delivery systems for nuclear weapons; and
- promote the health of the international economy, energy markets, and the environment.

CHINA'S CHALLENGE TO U.S. VITAL NATIONAL INTERESTS

Although Washington seeks a cooperative relationship with Beijing regarding nonproliferation, energy security, and the international economy and environment, the primary U.S. preoccupation regarding these national interests should be a rising China's systematic effort to undermine the second vital national interest mentioned—that is, to fundamentally alter the balance of power in Asia, diminish the vitality of the U.S.-Asian alliance system, and ultimately displace the United States as the Asian leader. Success in attaining these objectives would open the door to China's ability to undermine the first and third interests over time. As noted earlier, Beijing seeks to achieve these goals:

- replace the United States as the primary power in Asia;
- weaken the U.S. alliance system in Asia;[35]
- undermine the confidence of Asian nations in U.S. credibility, reliability, and staying power;
- use China's economic power to pull Asian nations closer to PRC geopolitical policy preferences;
- increase PRC military capability to strengthen deterrence against U.S. military intervention in the region;
- cast doubt on the U.S. economic model;
- ensure U.S. democratic values do not diminish the CCP's hold on domestic power; and
- avoid a major confrontation with the United States in the next decade.

President Xi signaled China's aims to undermine the Asian balance of power at the Conference on Interaction and Confidence Building Measures in Asia in early 2014 when he argued that "Asia's problems ultimately must be resolved by Asians and Asia's security ultimately must be protected by Asians."[36] The capacity of the United States to deal successfully with this systematic geoeconomic, military, and diplomatic challenge by China to U.S. primacy in Asia will determine the shape of the international order for decades to come.

THE RESPONSE OF U.S. GRAND STRATEGY TO CHINA'S STRATEGIC OBJECTIVES

The long-term U.S. effort to protect its vital national interests by integrating China into the international system is at serious risk today because Beijing has acquired the capacity, and increasingly displays the willingness, to pursue threatening policies against which American administrations have asserted they were hedging. Nevertheless, these same U.S. policymakers have continued to interact with China as if these dangerous Chinese policies were only theoretical and consigned to the distant future. In short, successive administrations have done much more cooperating with China than hedging, hoping that Beijing would gradually come to accept the United States' leading role in Asia despite all the evidence to the contrary, not least because cooperation was so much less costly in the short term than military, geoeconomic, and diplomatic hedging.

China has indeed become a rapidly growing economy, providing wealth and welfare gains both for itself and for American citizens, but it has acquired the wherewithal to challenge the United States, endangering the security of its allies and others in Asia, and to slowly chip away at the foundations of the liberal international order globally. In other words, China has not evolved into a "responsible stakeholder" as then Deputy Secretary of State Robert B. Zoellick called on it to become.[37] Instead, in recent decades Beijing has used the benign U.S. approach to the rise of Chinese power to strengthen its domestic economy, and thus the CCP's hold on power, to enhance its military capabilities and increase its diplomatic and geoeconomic sway in Asia and beyond, all while free-riding on the international order and public goods provided by the United States and its allies.

Therefore, the United States should become more strategically pro-active in meeting the Chinese challenge to U.S. interests and less preoc-cupied with how this more robust U.S. approach might be evaluated in Beijing. (The PRC apparently will remain convinced that Washington is practicing a containment policy no matter what policies the United States pursues.[38]) This means reconfiguring U.S. grand strategy toward China in the following four ways with consequent and systematic policy implementation:

- The United States should vitalize the U.S. economy at home, con-struct a new set of trading relationships in Asia that exclude China, fashion effective policies to deal with China's pervasive use of geo-economic tools in Asia and beyond, and, in partnership with U.S. allies and like-minded partners, create a new technology-control mechanism vis-à-vis China.[39]

- The United States should invest in U.S. defense capabilities and capacity to enable the United States to defeat China's emerging anti-access capabilities and permit successful U.S. power projection even against concerted opposition from Beijing.

- The United States should reinforce a new set of trusted strategic rela-tionships and partnerships throughout the Indo-Pacific region that include traditional U.S. alliances but go beyond them, pursuing as an explicit policy the objectives of both strengthening Asian states' ability to cope with China independently and building new forms of intra-Asian strategic cooperation that do not always involve, but will be systematically supported by, the United States.

- The United States should energize high-level diplomacy with China to attempt to mitigate the inherently profound tensions as the two nations pursue mutually incompatible grand strategies and to reas-sure U.S. allies and friends in Asia and beyond that its objective is to avoid a confrontation with China.

No U.S. grand strategy toward China can succeed without the con-tinuous involvement and leadership of President Barack Obama and his successors. Despite turmoil in the Middle East and tensions with Russia, the president should concentrate on managing the greatest stra-tegic challenge to the United States in the coming decades—the rise of Chinese power. His hands should be continually seen to be on the wheel of U.S. grand strategy toward China, and he should hold face-to-face meetings on the subject much more frequently with Asia's leaders and European Union heads of government. Occasional forty-five minute bilateral talks with his Asian counterparts at the margins of international meetings are insufficient to the task.

The same is true of Congress, which is an indispensable element in dealing with Chinese power over the long term. Partisan divides and the press of daily events will not excuse Congress if it largely ignores the effects of China's rise on U.S. interests. The congressional role in sustaining a successful U.S. grand strategy toward China is manifested primarily in three areas: giving the president trade-promotion authority so that he may quickly conclude the Trans-Pacific Partnership (TPP) free-trade agreements now being negotiated in Asia, reforming and providing the defense budgets necessary to maintain U.S. power projection and a credible Asian alliance system, and continuously holding U.S. administrations accountable for the implementation of their response to the rise of Chinese power.

Recommendations for U.S. Grand Strategy Toward China

To accomplish this robust U.S. grand strategy toward China, Washington should implement the following policies.

VITALIZE THE U.S. ECONOMY

Nothing would better promote the United States' strategic future and grand strategy toward China than robust economic growth in the United States.[40] Recent economic data suggests some optimism in that regard.[41] This must be the first priority of the president and the new Congress.

EXPAND ASIAN TRADE NETWORKS

- *Deliver on the Trans-Pacific Partnership.* The TPP until very recently has been conceived by the Obama administration primarily not as a geoeconomic answer to growing Chinese economic power and geopolitical coercion in Asia, but rather as a shot in the arm of a dying Doha Round at the World Trade Organization (WTO). Although, of course, the TPP will not erase China's asymmetrical economic advantages with respect to the nations of Asia, it will be a vivid demonstration that the United States is determined to compete on the Asian economic playing field. By the same token, U.S. grand strategy toward China will be seriously weakened without delivering on the TPP. A major push by the White House for ratification should therefore begin immediately in the new Congress and include seeking trade promotion authority. Many elements of U.S.-China economic interaction serve U.S. national interests and should be encouraged.[42] However, Beijing's constant challenges to the international trading system should be resisted and met with a unified response by the industrial democracies, led by the United States. Washington should continue to press Beijing to bring China's currency in line with its actual market value.

- *Fashion effective policies to deal with China's pervasive use of geoeconomic tools in Asia and beyond.* Never in history has one government so directly controlled so much wealth as does the leadership of China. It is not surprising, then, that as China's economic might has grown, so has its ability and inclination to use this power to advance geopolitical ends. China is often correctly described as the world's leading practitioner of geoeconomics. For the purposes of this report, geoeconomics is defined as "the use of economic instruments for geopolitical objectives."[43] This has been reflected in coercive geoeconomic Chinese policies toward Japan, ASEAN nations, and Australia, among others, with no serious U.S. policy response. A geoeconomic foreign policy approach would entail these initiatives:

  - U.S.-Asian alliances should be rebooted for offensive and defensive geoeconomic action. This intensified alliance focus should be as concentrated on geoeconomics as on political-military instruments.

  - The administration should construct a geoeconomic policy to deal with China over the long term, using the strength and positive power of the U.S. economy, innovation, and networks to attract Asian nations; and deal with the PRC's coercive pressure on its neighbors, in ways that are always consistent with an international rules-based system that is so obviously in the national interest of the United States and its friends and allies.

  - The U.S. energy revolution should be converted into lasting geopolitical gains in Asia by eliminating constraints on supplying U.S. allies and friends with gas and oil.

- *Create, in partnership with U.S. allies and like-minded partners, a new technology-control regime vis-à-vis Beijing.* Washington should pay increased attention to limiting China's access to advanced weaponry and militarily critical technologies. Although the United States certainly should lead the West in expanding international trade, this policy ought not to be extended to the point where it actually undermines American power and erodes Washington's ability to discharge its fundamental obligation to guarantee Asian and global security and meet the Chinese challenge. The virtues of enhanced trade with China "must not obscure the reality that deepening globalization increases Beijing's access to sophisticated weaponry and its associated elements," including through dual-use technologies.[44] Such acquisitions can undermine any American success in balancing China's rise with decisive and dangerous consequences.

Today, such capabilities obviously do not reside solely in the United States—they can be found in many nations, especially Washington's European and Asian allies. The United States should encourage these countries to develop a coordinated approach to constrict China's access to all technologies, including dual use, that can inflict "high-leverage strategic harm."[45] To establish a new technology regime toward China, Washington should enter into an immediate discussion with allies and friends with the aim of tightening restrictions on the sales of militarily critical technologies to China, including dual-use technologies. This will obviously not be easy to accomplish, but the effort should get under way immediately.

STRENGTHEN THE U.S. MILITARY

The United States should invest in defense capabilities and capacity specifically to defeat China's emerging anti-access capabilities and permit successful U.S. power projection even against concerted opposition from Beijing.

At present, the Obama administration's military component to strengthen U.S. power projection in Asia is small: adding a fourth attack submarine to Guam; rotating 2,500 marines to Darwin, Australia; putting a small number of littoral combat ships in Singapore; making minor improvements in technology, intelligence, and missile defense; and increasing U.S. naval forces in Asia from 50 percent to 60 percent over the long term.[46]

No nation in Asia, least of all China, will take seriously U.S. military enhancement in Asia unless the United States takes the following vigorous and comprehensive steps:

- Congress should remove sequestration caps and substantially increase the U.S. defense budget.[47]

- The White House should work with Congress on thoughtful, mean-ingful reform of the defense budget and force design. Absent that, the internal cost drivers (compensation and entitlements) within the budget will outpace any reasonable increase to the budget.

- The existing nuclear balance between the United States and China should be maintained, as it is crucial to the U.S. posture in Asia.

- Washington should accelerate U.S. military capabilities to coun-ter China's anti-access area denial (A2/AD) programs, especially in those areas where the United States retains advantage, such as stealthy long-range unmanned vehicles and undersea warfare.

- Washington should reiterate its insistence on freedom of navigation and overflight, including in exclusive economic zones, for military as well as civilian ships and planes, and challenge Beijing appropriately if those norms are violated.

- Washington should build military capability and capacity to increase interoperability with allies and partners in Asia to include aiding the regional states to develop their own A2/AD capabilities against China.

- Washington should accelerate the U.S. ballistic missile defense posture and network in the Pacific to support allies, among other objectives.

- Washington should enhance efforts to protect its space domain while developing an aerial alternative to space for high-volume communications.

- Washington should intensify a consistent U.S. naval and air presence in the South and East China Seas.

- Washington should increase the frequency and duration of naval exercises with South China Sea littoral states.

IMPLEMENT EFFECTIVE CYBER POLICIES

For the past decade, the United States has tolerated incessant cyber-attacks by China on the U.S. government, critical infrastructure, and businesses. Virtually nothing has been done to stop this cyber assault, and the "name and shame" approach toward China has clearly failed. (The U.S. indictment of five PLA officers, of course, had no impact on China's cyber espionage.) The Department of Defense cyber strategy published in 2011 announced a new doctrine, arguing that harmful action within the cyber domain can be met with a parallel response in another domain, known as equivalence.[48] No such equivalence has been exacted on China. Such passivity on the part of the United States should end, especially since there is no way to reach a verifiable cybersecurity agreement with China. The United States should implement the following cyber policies:

- Impose costs on China that are in excess of the benefits it receives from its violations in cyberspace. A good starting point is the recommendation of the Blair-Huntsman Commission of an across-the-board tariff on Chinese goods.[49]

- Increase U.S. offensive cyber capabilities to dissuade China's leaders from using cyberattacks against the United States and its partners in the region.

- Continue to improve U.S. cyber defenses. Securing cyberspace will require congressional action, including a law regulating information sharing between intelligence agencies and the corporate world.

- Pass relevant legislation in Congress, such as the Cyber Information Security Protection Act, allowing businesses to rapidly share intelligence on cyber threats with each other and the government without fear of lawsuits.

REINFORCE INDO-PACIFIC PARTNERSHIPS

The United States should reinforce a new web of partnerships throughout Asia that includes traditional U.S. alliances but goes beyond them, pursuing as an explicit policy the objectives of both strengthening Asian states to cope with China independently and building new forms of intra-Asian strategic cooperation that do not always involve, but will be systematically supported by, the United States.

The United States cannot defend its national interests in Asia without sustained support from its allies and friends. In one way or another, the PRC seeks to undermine each of these crucial bilateral relationships to test American strength and resilience in defending and promoting these ties in Northeast, Southeast, and South Asia. The first step in combating these corrosive Chinese efforts is to recognize that they are occurring; the second is to develop strategies to defeat them. At the same time, it is essential that Washington constantly reassure its democratic partners in Asia that it seeks to avoid a confrontation with China and that the steps delineated below are prudent in order to maintain the existing balance of power and to protect Western national interests in the Indo-Pacific.

- *Japan:* No other U.S. relationship approaches that with Japan in maintaining the current balance in Asia and dealing with the rise of Chinese power. Indeed, without close and enduring U.S.-Japan security cooperation, it is difficult to see how the United States could maintain its present power and influence in Asia. Thus, as Japan continues to emerge from its post–World War II self-imposed security constraints, the United States should continually support this crucial alliance partner by
  - substantially expanding its security relationship with Japan, encompassing all of Asia;
  - helping upgrade the Japan Self-Defense Forces (JSDF), including Japan's capabilities for joint/combined-arms/amphibious operations;
  - aligning concepts such as air-sea battle and dynamic defense through a dialogue with Japan on roles, missions, and capabilities;[50]
  - reinvigorating an extended deterrence dialogue with Japan;
  - intensifying ballistic missile defense (BMD) cooperation with Japan;
  - signaling more often that Japan remains fully and reliably under a U.S. security umbrella;
  - supporting Japan's cooperation with Vietnam, Australia, India, and other nations concerned with the rise of Chinese power; and
  - allowing liquefied natural gas exports to Japan.
- *South Korea:* The U.S. strategic relationship with the Republic of Korea (ROK) is essential to maintaining the balance of power in Asia. In that context, these bilateral ties should be reinforced by
  - ensuring adequate military capabilities are present on the Korean peninsula in the context of provocations from North Korea;
  - working with the ROK (and Japan) to develop a comprehensive strategy for regime change in North Korea;

- formulating with Seoul a shared vision for dealing with Korean unification;
- boosting the credibility of U.S.-extended nuclear guarantees to South Korea;
- increasing support for the ROK's BMD capabilities; and
- encouraging the ROK to eventually join the TPP.
- *Australia:* Australia is the southern anchor of U.S. relationships in the Pacific and, as a nation facing the Indian and Pacific Oceans, an essential link in U.S. Indo-Pacific strategy. The United States and Australia should cooperate to achieve the following goals:
  - The United States should use the Stirling naval base near Perth to support increased U.S. naval force structure in the region.
  - The United States should immediately accelerate cyber, space, and undersea cooperation with Australia.
  - The United States and Australia should jointly deploy surveillance aircraft and unmanned aerial vehicles on the Cocos Islands (Australian territory) in the Indian Ocean.
  - The two countries should work together to more rapidly identify potential Australian contributions to ballistic missile defense.
  - The scope and frequency of Australia's hosting of rotational deployments of U.S. military personnel should be increased.[51]
  - The U.S.-Australia free trade agreement should be upgraded, particularly as Australia progresses toward FTAs with Japan, Korea, and China.[52] Similarly, Australia should be included in the TPP.
  - Washington should support Australia's efforts to expand its strategic interaction with like-minded Asian nations.
- *India:* Especially in the face of an increasingly assertive China, the United States benefits from the presence of a robust democratic power that is willing to and capable of independently balancing Beijing's rising influence in Asia.[53] The United States should
  - substantially loosen its restraints on military technology transfer to India;
  - regard Indian nuclear weapons as an asset in maintaining the current balance of power in Asia;
  - markedly increase U.S.-India military-to-military cooperation, especially between the two navies;

- systemically assist India in building maritime capabilities in the Indian Ocean and beyond, including through substantial technology transfer;
- develop a global counterterrorism relationship with India;
- further incentivize India to sign defense cooperation agreements, including the Logistics Supply Agreement (LSA), the Communications Interoperability and Security Memorandum of Agreement (CISMOA), and the Basic Exchange and Cooperation Agreement for Geospatial Cooperation (BECA);
- advocate much more actively for India's long-pending request for membership in the Asia-Pacific Economic Cooperation (APEC) forum and in the global nonproliferation regimes; and
- vigorously support India's "Act East" policy to strengthen its power projection and influence into Southeast and East Asia.

- *Southeast Asia*: ASEAN nations are a primary target of China's geoeconomic coercion, not least regarding issues in the South China Sea. The United States should

- push harder for meaningful defense reform within the Armed Forces of the Philippines to develop a full range of defense capabilities that would enable the government to deter and prevent intrusions on or possible invasion of Philippine territory;
- boost Indonesia's role in joint exercises and expand its scope, symbolically indicative of Jakarta's growing centrality to security in the Asia Pacific, and gear military aid, training, and joint exercises with Indonesia toward air-sea capabilities;[54]
- help Singapore upgrade its current air force capabilities from F-16s to F-35s;
- encourage Malaysia to fully participate in the Proliferation Security Initiative, which it agreed to join in April 2014, and promote more active Malaysian involvement in combined exercises, domain awareness architectures, and the like;
- seek to expand the scope of activities during the annual U.S.-Vietnam naval exercises to include joint humanitarian assistance and disaster relief, and/or search and rescue exercises, and make more frequent stops at the port at Cam Ranh Bay in the short term;[55]
- establish strategic International Military Exchange Training (IMET) programs with Myanmar, with a focus on professionalizing the

military, and continue to integrate the Myanmar military into, and expand its participation in, joint international military exercises;[56]

- advocate substantial IMET expansion throughout Southeast Asia; and
- help build domestic democratic political capacity throughout the region.
- *Taiwan:* A comprehensive, durable, and unofficial relationship between Taiwan and the United States should be a feature of an invigorated U.S. grand strategy toward China, including through the legislative framework of the Taiwan Relations Act (TRA). The United States should reaffirm its military commitment to Taiwan by upholding TRA obligations to "provide Taiwan with arms of a defensive character." Possible future arms sales to Taiwan could include signals intelligence aircraft, transport aircraft, upgraded engines for F-16s, upgrades to frigates and other ships, and/or land-based missile defense systems.[57]

ENERGIZE HIGH-LEVEL DIPLOMACY WITH BEIJING

The United States should energize high-level diplomacy with China to attempt to mitigate the inherently profound tensions as the two nations pursue mutually incompatible grand strategies, and to reassure U.S. allies and friends in Asia and beyond that Washington is doing everything it can to avoid a confrontation with Beijing.

Despite the destabilizing objectives of China's grand strategy in Asia and in the context of implementing the many policy recommendations in this report to systemically strengthen the American response to the rise of Chinese power, the United States bears major responsibilities to promote international stability, prosperity, and peace—in Asia and across the globe.

In this context, take into account the negative consequences for each country's formidable domestic challenges if the United States and China seriously mismanage their relationship. Imagine the tumultuous effects on the global economy. Consider the dramatic increase in tension throughout Asia and the fact that no country in this vast region wants to have to choose between China and the United States. Envision the corrosive impact on U.S.-China collaboration on climate change.

Picture the fallout over attempts to deal with the nuclear weapons programs of North Korea and Iran.

With this in mind, the U.S.-China discourse should be more
candid, high level, and private than current practice—no rows of officials principally trading sermons across the table in Washington or
Beijing. Bureaucracies wish to do today what they did yesterday, and
wish to do tomorrow what they did today. It is, therefore, inevitable
that representatives from Washington and Beijing routinely mount
bills of indictment regarding the other side. All are familiar with these
calcified and endlessly repeated talking points. As the Chinese prov-
erb puts it, "To talk much and arrive nowhere is the same as climbing
a tree to catch a fish."

For such an intensified high-level bilateral dialogue between Washington and Beijing to be fruitful, it should avoid concentrating primarily on the alleged perfidious behavior of the other side. For instance,
no amount of American condemnation of China's human rights prac-
tices—private or by megaphone—will consequentially affect Beijing's
policies, including toward Hong Kong, and no degree of Chinese com-
plaints will lead the United States to weaken its alliance systems that
are indispensable to the protection of its vital national interests. Nor
is it likely that either side will admit to its actual grand strategy toward
the other. In any case, endemic contention will over time contribute to
a systemic worsening of U.S.-China bilateral relations that results in all
the destructive consequences enumerated earlier.

Instead, after thorough consultations with its Asian allies, the United
States should commit to working with China on two or three issues that
would make a positive contribution to bilateral ties and to international
peace and security. After the November 2014 U.S.-China summit in
Beijing, Asian security would be good subject with which to begin. For
example, subjects for joint exploration could include the possibility of
creating a version of the Organization for Security and Cooperation in
Europe for Asia, expanding the talks on North Korea to include broader
Asian security issues, or agreeing on enhanced security confidence-
building measures between the two sides. To inspire fresh thinking and
creative policy initiatives, it might be best if the senior individuals to
take the lead in these talks were not in the direct national security chain
of command.

Bipartisan candidates for such a U.S. team include Thomas Donilon,
former Obama national security advisor, and Robert Zoellick, former

World Bank president and George W. Bush administration policy-maker. The Chinese side would have similar credentials and all these individuals would, of course, need the confidence of their respective leaders. Such a channel would simply recognize the reality that the two countries' strategic policies are being primarily designed not by foreign and defense ministries, but by those close to each president and by the presidents themselves, and that the current means of bilateral interaction are not adequate for the task.

Conclusion

Policy experts critical of the grand strategy toward China proposed in this report will likely fall into at least six categories. First, some will argue that China has no grand strategy. Although there may be those in Beijing who disagree with China's current strategic approach, its dominating elements are not a mystery. Chinese officials insistently argue that the U.S. alliance system in Asia is a product of the Cold War and should be dismantled; that the United States' Asian allies and friends should loosen their U.S. ties and that failure to do so will inevitably produce a negative PRC reaction; that U.S. efforts to maintain its current presence and power in Asia are dimensions of an American attempt to contain China and therefore must be condemned and resisted; that U.S. military power projection in the region is dangerous and should be reduced (even as the PLA continues to build up its military capabilities with the clear objective of reducing U.S. military options in the context of a U.S.-China confrontation); and that the U.S. economic model is fundamentally exploitative and should have no application in Asia. To not take seriously official Chinese government statements along these lines is to not take China seriously. That Beijing does not hope to realize these policy goals in the short term does not reduce their potential undermining effect in the decades ahead. In short, if China were to achieve the policy objectives contained in these official statements, it would clearly replace the United States as Asia's leading power. If that does not represent a PRC grand strategy, what would?

Second, some may say that the analysis and policy recommendations in this report are too pessimistic, based on a worst-case appraisal of Chinese behavior. To the contrary, we draw our conclusions from China's current actions regarding its internal and external security, its neighbors, and U.S. presence in Asia. We project nothing that is not already apparent in China's present policies and strategic intentions. Nevertheless, this hardly represents the worst case if China began to behave like the Soviet Union, necessitating something far more costly than balancing. The word "containment" comes to mind, and we certainly do not recommend that vis-à-vis China in current circumstances, not least because no Asian nation would join in such an endeavor.

Other policymakers might argue that China's international behavior is "normal" for a rising power, that China is gradually being socialized into the international system and it is far too early for Washington to give up on comprehensive cooperation and strategic reassurance toward Beijing. The issue here is how long the United States should pursue a policy toward China that is clearly not sufficiently protecting U.S. vital national interests. Although Beijing has in general acted responsibly in the international lending institutions and may be slowly moving toward progress on difficult issues (such as climate change), Kurt Campbell, former State Department assistant secretary for East Asian and Pacific affairs in the Obama administration, recently stressed, "We were always looking for deeper cooperation with China and attempts to have on-the-ground cooperation—for example, on aid or humanitarian support operations, we weren't able to bring about; in military-to-military relations, on the diplomatic agenda, on aid, we found it very difficult to get meaningful results."[58]

"Meaningful results" have been so difficult to achieve in the U.S.-China relationship precisely because China seeks to replace the United States as the leading power in Asia. And although Chinese behavior may be "normal" for a rising nation, that does not diminish China's overall negative impact on the balance of power in the vast Indo-Pacific region; nor does it reduce the crucial requirement for Washington to develop policies that meet this challenge of the rise of Chinese power and thwart Beijing's objective to systematically undermine American strategic primacy in Asia.

Fourth, some may assert that China's integration into the international system broadly serves important U.S. purposes, binds Beijing to a rules-based system and increases the costs to the PRC of going against it, and thus should trump other U.S. concerns about China's internal and external behavior. We accept that integrating China into international institutions will continue and that the United States will accrue some benefits from that activity. Our argument is that basing U.S. grand strategy primarily on such Chinese global integration ignores the strategic reality that China has made far greater relative gains through such processes than the United States has over the past three decades, that China has accordingly increased its national power in ways that potentially deeply threaten U.S. national interests in the long term, and that therefore the United States needs to understand and internalize this disturbing fact and respond to such PRC international assimilation with much more robust American policies and power projection into Asia.

Fifth, critics may also say that the United States' Asian allies and friends will never go along with the grand strategy outlined in this document. This concern seems to concentrate not on the merits of our strategic approach, but rather on its reception in the region. In any case, what the allies want is not to cut ties with China, but rather increased U.S. capabilities in the region, increased reassurance of American protection, and increased U.S. support for their own economic growth and security. The grand strategy outlined in this report advances all of these objectives. Moreover, it is difficult to exaggerate the current anxiety among virtually all Asian nations about the strategic implications of the rise of Chinese power, recent examples of PRC aggressiveness in the East and South China Seas, and the conviction that only the United States can successfully deter Beijing's corrosive strategic ambitions. Because of PRC behavior, Asian states have already begun to balance against China through greater intra-Asian cooperation—actions that are entirely consistent with and only reinforce our U.S. grand strategy. Indeed, the worry across Asia today is not that the United States will pursue overly robust policies toward China; rather, it is that Washington is insufficiently aware of Beijing's ultimate disruptive strategic goals in Asia, is periodically attracted to a G2 formula, and may not be up to the challenge of effectively dealing with the rise of China over the long term. These deeply worried views across Asian governments are fertile ground on which to plant a revised U.S. grand strategy toward China.

Moreover, a close examination of the specific policy prescriptions in this study reveal few that would not be welcomed by the individual nations of Asia to which they apply. Although this major course correction by the United States toward China would not gain allied endorsement overnight, with sustained and resolute U.S. presidential leadership and the immense leverage the United States has with its Asian allies and friends, this is not too steep a strategic hill to climb, especially given the profound U.S. national interests at stake across Asia. Finally, nothing in this grand strategy requires the United States and its allies to diminish their current economic and political cooperation with China. Rather, the emphasis is on developing those U.S. and allied components that are ultimately necessary to make this cooperation sustainable. In other words, if the balance of power alters fundamentally, U.S. and Asian economic cooperation with China could not be maintained.

Finally, the question arises regarding how China will respond to the U.S. grand strategy recommended here. Are not the risks of pursuing this grand strategy too great? One could certainly expect a strong Chinese reaction and a sustained chill in the bilateral relationship, including fewer meetings among senior officials, little progress on bilateral economic issues, less opportunities for American business in China, reduced military-to-military interaction, a reduction in societal interchange, and perhaps fewer Chinese students in American universities. (We dismiss the likelihood that China would respond to the measures recommended in this report by selling off its U.S. bond holdings because of the consequential reduction in their value.) These steps by Beijing would not be trivial but also would not threaten vital U.S. national interests. If China went further in its policy as opposed to reacting rhetorically, the more aggressive Beijing's policy response and the more coercive its actions, the more likely that America's friends and allies in Asia would move even closer to Washington. We do not think that China will find an easy solution to this dilemma.

Moreover, it is likely that Beijing would continue to cooperate with the United States in areas that it thinks serve China's national interests—on the global economy, international trade, climate change, counterterrorism, the Iranian nuclear weapons program, North Korea, and post-2016 Afghanistan. Put differently, we do not think the Chinese leadership in a fit of pique—hardly in China's strategic tradition—would act in ways that damage its policy purposes and its reputation around Asia. In short, this strategic course correction in U.S. policy toward China would certainly trigger a torrent of criticism from Beijing because it would begin to systemically address China's goal of dominating Asia and produce a more cantankerous PRC in the UN Security Council, but it would not end many aspects of U.S.-China international collaboration based on compatible national interests. Although there are risks in following the course proposed here, as with most fundamental policy departures, such risks are substantially smaller than those that are increasing because of an inadequate U.S. strategic response to the rise of Chinese power.

In any case, there is no reason why a China that did not seek to overturn the balance of power in Asia should object to the policy prescriptions contained in this report. And which of the policy prescriptions would those who wish to continue the current prevailing U.S. approach to China—that is, cooperation—reject? In short, these measures do not "treat China as an enemy" as some American analysts rightfully warn against; rather, they seek to protect vital U.S. and allied national interests, a reasonable and responsible objective.

Washington simply cannot have it both ways—to accommodate Chinese concerns regarding U.S. power projection into Asia through "strategic reassurance" and at the same time to promote and defend U.S. vital national interests in this vast region. It is, of course, the second that must be at the core of a successful U.S. grand strategy toward China.

In this same sense, there is no real prospect of building fundamental trust, "peaceful coexistence," "mutual understanding," a strategic partnership, or a "new type of major country relations" between the United States and China. Rather, the most that can be hoped for is caution and restrained predictability by the two sides as intense U.S.-China strategic competition becomes the new normal, and even that will be no easy task to achieve in the period ahead. The purpose of U.S. diplomacy in these dangerous circumstances is to mitigate and manage the severe inherent tensions between these two conflicting strategic paradigms, but it cannot hope to eliminate them. Former Australian Prime Minister and distinguished sinologist Kevin Rudd believes the Chinese may have come to the same conclusion: "There is emerging evidence to suggest that President Xi, now two years into his term, has begun to conclude that the long-term strategic divergences between U.S. and Chinese interests make it impossible to bring about any fundamental change in the relationship."[59]

The Obama administration has clearly pursued a policy approach far different than the one recommended in this report. To be clear, this involves a more fundamental issue than policy implementation. All signs suggest that President Obama and his senior colleagues have a profoundly different and much more benign diagnosis of China's strategic objectives in Asia than do we. Like some of its predecessors, the Obama administration has not appeared to understand and digest the reality that China's grand strategy in Asia in this era is designed to undermine U.S. vital national interests and that it has been somewhat successful in that regard. It is for this overriding reason that the Obama team has continued the cooperate-but-hedge policy of its predecessors, but with much greater emphasis on cooperating than on hedging.

Many of these omissions in U.S. policy would seem to stem from an administration worried that such actions would offend Beijing and therefore damage the possibility of enduring strategic cooperation between the two nations, thus the dominating emphasis on cooperation. That self-defeating preoccupation by the United States based on a long-term goal of U.S.-China strategic partnership that cannot be accomplished in the foreseeable future should end.

The profound test that the rise of Chinese power represents for the United States is likely to last for decades. It is unrealistic to imagine that China's grand strategy toward the United States will evolve in a way—at least in the next ten years—that accepts American power and influence as linchpins of Asian peace and security, rather than seeks to systematically diminish them. Thus, the central question concerning the future of Asia is whether the United States will have the political will; the geoeconomic, military, and diplomatic capabilities; and, crucially, the right grand strategy to deal with China to protect vital U.S. national interests.

Endnotes

1. Edward Mead Earle, ed., *Makers of Modern Strategy: Military Thought from Machiavelli to Hitler* (Princeton, NJ: Princeton University Press, 1943), p. viii.
2. Ibid.
3. Ibid.
4. Melvyn Leffler, "Containment," in Silvio Pons and Robert Service, eds., *A Dictionary of 20th-Century Communism* (Princeton, NJ: Princeton University Press, 2012), p. 236.
5. "Excerpts from Pentagon's Plan: 'Prevent the Re-Emergence of a New Rival," *New York Times*, March 8, 1992.
6. The logic of restricting trade during the Cold War has been carefully analyzed in Joanne Gowa, *Allies, Adversaries and International Trade* (Princeton, NJ: Princeton University Press, 1994). For a comprehensive list of all the agreements entered into by the United States, see U.S. Congress, House Committee on Foreign Affairs, *Collective Defense Treaties, with Maps, Texts of Treaties, a Chronology, Status of Forces Agreements, and Comparative Chart* (Washington: U.S. Government Printing Office, 1967). A broader discussion of the network of military bases in the Cold War can be found in Allan R. Millet and Peter Maslowski, *For the Common Defense* (New York: The Free Press, 1984), pp. 471–541. The United States' global campaign against Soviet ideology is examined in Nicholas J. Cull, *The Cold War and the United States Information Agency: American Propaganda and Public Diplomacy, 1945–1989* (Cambridge: Cambridge University Press, 2009). For a discussion of the United States' policies to maintain scientific and industrial superiority during the period while guarding against becoming a garrison state, see Audra J. Wolfe, *Science, Technology, and the State in the Cold War* (Baltimore, MD: Johns Hopkins University Press, 2013); and Aaron L. Friedberg, *In the Shadow of the Garrison State* (Princeton, NJ: Princeton University Press, 2000).
7. For a further discussion of this concept, see Ashley J. Tellis, "China's Grand Strategy: The Quest for Comprehensive National Power and Its Consequences," in Gary Schmitt, ed., *The Rise of China: Essays on the Future Competition* (New York: Encounter Books, 2009).
8. Alastair Iain Johnson, "Cultural Realism and Strategy in Maoist China," in Peter J. Katzenstein, ed., *The Culture of National Security: Norms and Identity in World Politics* (New York: Columbia University Press, 1996), p. 267.
9. For further analysis on the connection between the "century of humiliation" and China's current geopolitical strategy, see Orville Schell and John Delury, *Wealth and Power: China's Long March to the Twenty-First Century* (New York: Random House, 2013); and Zheng Wang, *Never Forget National Humiliation: Historical Memory in Chinese Politics and Foreign Relations* (New York: Columbia University Press, 2012).
10. Ye Zicheng, *Inside China's Grand Strategy: The Perspective from the People's Republic* (Lexington: University Press of Kentucky, 2011), p. 72.
11. For an illuminating discussion, see Christopher A. Ford, *The Mind of Empire: China's History and Modern Foreign Relations* (Lexington: University Press of Kentucky, 2010).

12. Wang Gungwu, "Early Ming Relations with Southeast Asia: A Background Essay," in John K. Fairbank, ed., *The Chinese World Order: Traditional China's Foreign Relations* (Cambridge, MA: Harvard University Press, 1968), p. 61.

13. Henry Kissinger, *World Order* (New York: Penguin Press, 2014), p. 213.

14. Michael D. Swaine and Ashley J. Tellis, *Interpreting China's Grand Strategy: Past, Present, and Future* (Santa Monica, CA: RAND Corporation, 2001), p. 16.

15. "Full text: China's new party chief Xi Jinping's speech," BBC News China, November 15, 2012, http://www.bbc.com/news/world-asia-china-20338586.

16. See Communiqué on the Current State of the Ideological Sphere, "A Notice from the Central Committee of the Communist Party of China's General Office," April 22, 2013, http://www.chinafile.com/document-9-chinafile-translation.

17. For a discussion of Mao's personality and his leadership, see Lucian W. Pye, "Mao Tse-tung's Leadership Style," *Political Science Quarterly* vol. 91, no. 2, summer 1976, pp. 219–35. For an overview of the Red Guard movement, see Juliana P. Heaslet, "The Red Guards: Instruments of Destruction in the Cultural Revolution," *Asian Survey* vol. 12, no. 12, December 1972, pp. 1032–47.

18. Elizabeth C. Economy, "China's Imperial President," *Foreign Affairs*, November/December 2014.

19. "A New Workshop of the World," *Economist*, October 10, 2002.

20. John Williamson, "Is the 'Beijing Consensus' Now Dominant?," *Asia Policy* no. 13, January 2012, pp. 1–16.

21. For an extended discussion of the tensions between relative and absolute gains that motivate the geopolitical response to China, see Ashley J. Tellis, *Balancing Without Containment: An American Strategy for Managing China* (Washington, DC: Carnegie Endowment for International Peace, 2014), pp. 29–32.

22. James Mann, *The China Fantasy: Why Capitalism Will Not Bring Democracy to China* (New York: Penguin Books, 2008).

23. See the insightful discussion in Daniel W. Drezner, "Bad Debts: Assessing China's Financial Influence in Great Power Politics," *International Security* vol. 34, no. 2, fall 2009, pp. 7–45.

24. See Lant Pritchett and Lawrence Summers on the inevitable dramatic slowing of the Chinese economy. "Asiaphoria Meets Regression to the Mean," NBER Working Paper no. 20573 (Cambridge, MA: National Bureau of Economic Research, October 2014). They may well be right, but who predicted thirty-plus years of China's double-digit growth?

25. Michael R. Chambers, "Rising China: The Search for Power and Plenty," in Ashley J. Tellis and Michael Wills, eds., *Strategic Asia 2006-07: Trade, Interdependence, and Security* (Seattle, WA: National Bureau of Asian Research, 2006), p. 76.

26. The many dimensions of China's cooptation of Russia are surveyed in James A. Bellacqua, *The Future of China-Russia Relations* (Lexington: University Press of Kentucky, 2010).

27. For details and the larger strategic implications of the "decoupling" of the United States and Asia portended by this modernization, see Ashley J. Tellis and Travis Tanner, *Strategic Asia 2012–13: China's Military Modernization* (Seattle, WA: National Bureau of Asian Research, 2013).

28. David Cohen, "'Development is the Key to Peace': Chinese Leaders Discuss Future of Asia," in *China Brief* vol. 14, no. 10, May 23, 2014.

29. David Shambaugh, *China Goes Global: The Partial Power* (New York: Oxford University Press, 2013).

30. Henry Kissinger, "Avoiding a U.S.-China Cold War," *Washington Post*, January 14, 2011.

31. Mann, *The China Fantasy*, pp. 101–12.

32. Catherine L. Mann, "Breaking Up Is Hard to Do: Global Co-Dependency, Collective Action, and the Challenges of Global Adjustment," *CESifo Forum*, January 2005, http://petersoninstitute.org/publications/papers/manno105b.pdf.

33. For an extended discussion of these alternatives, their strengths, and their limitations from an American perspective, see Ashley J. Tellis, "The Geopolitics of the TTIP and the TTP: Geo-economic Containment of China?," in Sanjaya Baru, ed., *Power Shifts and New Blocs in the Global Trading System* (London: International Institute for Strategic Studies, 2015); Tellis, *Balancing Without Containment*, pp. 4–25.

34. See Robert Ellsworth, Andrew Goodpaster, and Rita Hauser, co-chairs, *America's National Interests: A Report from The Commission on America's National Interests, 2000* (Washington, DC: Commission on America's National Interests, July 2000).

35. Note these Chinese comments on the subject: "US needs to rein in destabilizing Japanese nationalism: Xinhua," *Want China Times*, December 4, 2013, http://www.wantchinatimes.com/news-subclass-cnt.aspx?id=20131204000059&cid=1101; Ren Zhongxi, "Xinhua Focus: Right-leaning Japan becomes Washington's liability in Asia-Pacific," *CCTV*, April 23, 2014, http://english.cntv.cn/2014/04/23/ARTI1398262842351527.shtml; Chen Jimin, "America's Rebalance Strategy and Challenges for China," *Study Times*, February 9, 2015, http://www.qstheory.cn/international/2015-02/09/c_1114300613.htm; Dai Bingguo's comments to then Secretary of State Hillary Clinton ("Why don't you just 'pivot' out of here?") in *Hard Choices* (New York: Simon & Schuster, 2014), p. 79; Zhong Sheng, "Hold mainstream of China-ASEAN relations," *People's Daily*, April 6, 2012, http://www.chinadaily.com.cn/opinion/2012-04/09/content_15004996.htm; "A Neutral U.S. helpful to stability in South China Sea," *China Daily*, July 5, 2012, http://usa.chinadaily.com.cn/opinion/2012-05/07/content_15226749.htm; "Foreign Ministry Spokesperson Liu Weimin's Regular Press Conference on June 4, 2012," http://www.chinaconsulate.org.nz/eng/fyrth/t939675.htm; "U.S. will not backtrack on rebalance toward Asia: envoy," *Xinhua*, July 23, 2013, http://news.xinhuanet.com/english/world/2013-07/23/c_132564914.htm.

36. Xi Jinping, "New Asian security concept for new progress in security cooperation," remarks at the Fourth Summit of the Conference on Interaction and Confidence Building Measures in Asia, Shanghai, May 21, 2014.

37. "Whither China: From Membership to Responsibility?" remarks by Robert Zoellick for the National Committee on U.S.-China Relations, New York City, September 21, 2005.

38. As Chinese Minister of Defense General Chang Wanquan noted, "With the latest developments in China, it can never be contained." Major General Luo Yuan, known for his hawkish views, encouraged Chinese "vigilance" as the United States continues to "bolster its five major military alliances in the Asia-Pacific region, adjusts the position of its five major military base clusters, and seeks more entry rights for military bases around China." Other official statements reference perceived U.S. efforts at containing Beijing in calls for "more cooperation and less containment," requiring Washington to "discard its containment fantasy [and] treat China equally and fairly." Academic analyses also point to Chinese concerns that the United States is constructing a "super long line of defense" stretching from the Aleutian Islands to the Persian Gulf with the sole aim of containing China (Lyle J. Goldstein, "How China Sees America's Moves in Asia: Worse Than Containment," *National Interest*, October 29, 2014; Zhou Jinghao, "U.S. Containment Frays China's Nerves," *Global Times*, November 25, 2013; Luo Jun, "U.S. needs to discard containment fantasy," *Xinhua*, June 1, 2014; "Hagel to Meet Xi as China Vows No Compromising on Sea Disputes," *Bloomberg Businessweek*, April 9, 2014; "China top military paper warns U.S. aims to contain rise," *Reuters*, January 10, 2012; "CPPCC calls for less containment in Sino-US ties," *CCTV*, March 3, 2010).

39. See, e.g., Dennis Blair and Jon Huntsman, co-chairs, "The IP Commission Report: The Report of the Commission on the Theft of American Intellectual Property," National Bureau of Asian Research, May 2013, http://www.ipcommission.org/report/ip_commission_report_052213.pdf.

40. As Richard N. Haass notes, "The United States is fast approaching one of those truly historic turning points: either it will act to get its fiscal house in order, thereby restoring the prerequisites of this country's primacy, or it will fail to and, as a result, suffer both the domestic and international consequences." He further highlights five elements central to restoring America's strength at home: reducing the federal deficit and ratio of national debt to GDP; putting into place a comprehensive energy strategy; improving the quality of education; upgrading domestic physical infrastructure; and modernizing outdated immigration policy. Richard N. Haass, *Foreign Policy Begins at Home: The Case for Putting America's House in Order* (New York: Basic Books, 2014), p. 124. A similar discussion is found in Kim Holmes, *Rebound: Getting America Back to Great* (New York: Rowman & Littlefield, 2013).

41. Evidence about American economic power gathered by Goldman Sachs is found in its January 2015 outlook, "U.S. Preeminence." "From the peak before the 2008 financial crisis, the U.S. economy has grown a further 8.1 percent in real terms, compared with declines of 2.2 percent for the Eurozone and 1.1 percent for Japan. The gap between GDP growth rates in fast-rising emerging-market economies and the United States shrank from 6.5 percentage points in 2007 to 2.6 points in 2014, and it's expected to narrow further this year to 1.2 points as China slows. The gains are even more striking when examining business statistics. The debt leverage of listed U.S. companies is lower than that of firms in any of its trading partners. U.S. labor productivity is substantially higher than that of the Eurozone, Japan or any emerging-market country. In terms of average manufacturing costs, the U.S. has an advantage over every one of the ten largest exporters, except China." See also David Ignatius, "In foreign policy, play to American strength," *Washington Post*, February 8, 2015; Goldman Sachs Investment Management Division, "Outlook: US Preeminence," January 2015.

42. As Walter Lohman, director of the Heritage Foundation's Asian Studies Center puts it, "In the end, fostering a global economy growing on liberal principles and institutions is one of the most potent policies to counter China's national aims. China cannot avoid the laws of economics forever. It must resolve the fundamental contradiction between maintaining high growth and real free-market reform. Time is on our side in that regard because regional and ultimately global liberalization and the consequent growth are the most powerful inducements to reform" (interview with the authors, 2014).

43. Robert D. Blackwill and Jennifer M. Harris, *Geoeconomics and Statecraft*, forthcoming.

44. Ashley J. Tellis, *Balancing Without Containment: An American Strategy for Managing China* (Washington, DC: Carnegie Endowment for International Peace, 2014), p. 52.

45. A 1990 U.S. Department of Defense policy persuasively argued this should be the benchmark for deciding whether a particular military technology should be considered destabilizing.

46. Bill Gertz, "Inside the Ring: Pentagon reevaluating pivot to Asia," *Washington Times*, March 5, 2014.

47. The Pentagon should focus its budget on the military pivot to the Pacific, which means continued investments in high-end weapons, including the F-35 Joint Strike Fighter or the new Long-Range Strike Bomber. Base realignment and closure authority, as well as smart reforms targeted at compensation and overhead costs, should also be implemented. For other sensible recommendations on increasing the U.S. defense budget, see Diem Nguyen Salmon, "A Proposal for the FY 2016 Defense Budget," Heritage

Foundation Backgrounder #2989, January 30, 2015; Ashton B. Carter, "Running the Pentagon Right," *Foreign Affairs*, January/February 2014; Ron Haskins and Michael O'Hanlon, "Stop Sequestering Defense," *Defense News*, October 13, 2014; Michèle Flournoy and Eric Edelman, "Cuts to defense spending are hurting national security," *Washington Post*, September 19, 2014; "The Pentagon's 2016 Budget Will Focus on the Pacific," *Defense One*, December 5, 2014; and Nicholas Burns and Jonathon Price, eds., *The Future of American Defense* (Washington, DC: Aspen Institute, 2014).

48. Department of Defense Strategy for Operating in Cyberspace, July 2011.

49. See Gordon Chang, "Only Tariffs Will Stop China's Cyber Attacks," *World Affairs Journal*, October 23, 2014; Blair and Huntsman, "The IP Commission Report."

50. Richard L. Armitage and Joseph S. Nye, "The U.S.-Japan Alliance: Anchoring Stability in Asia," August 2012, p. 17. Also see Michael Green and Nicholas Szechenyi, eds., "Pivot 2.0," Center for Strategic and International Studies, January 2015; Sheila Smith, "A Strategy for the U.S.-Japan Alliance," Council on Foreign Relations Press, April 2012; Sheila Smith, "Feeling the Heat: Asia's Shifting Geopolitics and the U.S.-Japan Alliance," *World Politics Review*, July 9, 2013.

51. Australian Minister for Foreign Affairs Julie Bishop, "U.S.-Australia: The Alliance in an Emerging Asia," speech delivered at the Center for Strategic and International Studies, Washington, DC, January 22, 2014.

52. Original FTA text available from the Office of the U.S. Trade Representative; also see Australian Department of Foreign Affairs and Trade, "Trans-Pacific Partnership Agreement negotiations."

53. Ashley J. Tellis, "Productive but Joyless? Narendra Modi and U.S.-India Relations," Carnegie Endowment for International Peace, May 12, 2014, http://carnegieendowment.org/2014/05/12/productive-but-joyless-narendra-modi-and-u.s.-india-relations.

54. Murray Hiebert, Ted Osius, and Gregory B. Poling, "A U.S.-Indonesia Partnership for 2020: Recommendations for Forging a 21st Century Relationship," Center for Strategic and International Studies, September 2013.

55. Murray Hiebert, Phuong Nguyen, and Gregory B. Poling, "A New Era in U.S.-Vietnam Relations: Deepening Ties Two Decades After Normalization," Center for Strategic and International Studies, June 2014.

56. "U.S.-Burma Relations: Peace, Stability, and the Transition to Democracy," Policy Task Force from the Henry M. Jackson School of International Studies, 2013.

57. Shirley A. Kan, "Taiwan: Major U.S. Arms Sales Since 1990," Congressional Research Service, August 29, 2014, p. 26.

58. James Massola, "Barack Obama's China Policy Has Not Been Successful, Says US Official," *Sydney Morning Herald*, November 2, 2014.

59. Kevin Rudd, "East Asia's Strategic and Economic Future: Chinese Perspectives and American Responses," address at the launch of the Zbigniew K. Brzezinski Institute at the Center for Strategic and International Studies, Washington, DC, October 1, 2014.

About the Authors

Robert D. Blackwill is Henry A. Kissinger senior fellow for U.S. foreign policy at the Council on Foreign Relations (CFR). Previously, he was senior fellow at the RAND Corporation in Santa Monica, California, from 2008 to 2010, after serving from 2004 to 2008 as president of BGR International. As deputy assistant to the president and deputy national security advisor for strategic planning under President George W. Bush, Blackwill was responsible for government-wide policy planning to help develop and coordinate the mid- and long-term direction of American foreign policy. He also served as presidential envoy to Iraq and was the administration's coordinator for U.S. policies regarding Afghanistan and Iran. Blackwill went to the National Security Council (NSC) after serving as the U.S. ambassador to India from 2001 to 2003, and he is the recipient of the 2007 Bridge-Builder Award for his role in transforming U.S.-India relations.

Prior to reentering government in 2001, Blackwill was the Belfer lecturer in international security at the Harvard Kennedy School. From 1989 to 1990, Blackwill was special assistant to President George H.W. Bush for European and Soviet affairs, during which time he was awarded the Commander's Cross of the Order of Merit by the Federal Republic of Germany for his contribution to German unification. Earlier in his career, he was the U.S. ambassador to conventional arms negotiations with the Warsaw Pact, director for European affairs at the NSC, principal deputy assistant secretary of state for political-military affairs, and principal deputy assistant secretary of state for European affairs. Blackwill is author and editor of many articles and books on transatlantic relations, Russia and the West, the Greater Middle East, and Asian security. He edited the CFR book *Iran: The Nuclear Challenge* (June 2012). His book, a best seller coauthored with Graham Allison of the Harvard Kennedy School, is titled *Lee Kuan Yew: The Grand Master's Insights on China, the United States, and the World* (MIT Press,

February 2013). He is coauthor of a forthcoming book with Jennifer M. Harris, *Geoeconomics and Statecraft*. He is a member of the Council on Foreign Relations, the International Institute for Strategic Studies, the Trilateral Commission, and the Aspen Strategy Group, and is on the board of Harvard University's Belfer Center for Science and International Affairs.

Ashley J. Tellis is a senior associate at the Carnegie Endowment for International Peace, specializing in international security, defense, and Asian strategic issues. While on assignment to the U.S. Department of State as senior advisor to the undersecretary of state for political affairs, he was intimately involved in negotiating the civil nuclear agreement with India. Previously, he was commissioned into the U.S. Foreign Service and served as senior advisor to the ambassador at the U.S. Embassy in New Delhi. He also served on the National Security Council staff as special assistant to the president and senior director for strategic planning and Southwest Asia. Prior to his government service, Tellis was senior policy analyst at the RAND Corporation and professor of policy analysis at the Frederick S. Pardee RAND Graduate School. He is the author of *India's Emerging Nuclear Posture* (2001) and coauthor of *Interpreting China's Grand Strategy: Past, Present, and Future* (2000). He is the research director of the strategic Asia program at the National Bureau of Asian Research and coeditor of the program's eleven most recent annual volumes, including this year's *Strategic Asia 2014–15: U.S. Alliances and Partnerships at the Center of Global Power.* His academic publications, which include numerous Carnegie and RAND reports, have appeared in many edited volumes and journals, and he is frequently called to testify before Congress. Tellis is a member of several professional organizations related to defense and international studies, including the Council on Foreign Relations, the International Institute for Strategic Studies, the United States Naval Institute, and the Navy League of the United States.

Study Group on U.S. Grand Strategy Toward China

Graham T. Allison
*Belfer Center for Science
and International Affairs*

Alyssa Ayres, *ex officio*
Council on Foreign Relations

Robert D. Blackwill, *ex officio*
Council on Foreign Relations

Elisabeth Bumiller
New York Times

Richard R. Burt
McLarty Associates

Richard C. Bush III
Brookings Institution

James E. Cartwright
Center for Strategic and International Studies

Victor Cha
Edmund A. Walsh School of Foreign Service

Jerome A. Cohen
New York University School of Law

Richard N. Cooper
Harvard University

Richard Danzig
Center for a New American Security

John Deutch
Massachusetts Institute of Technology

Daniel W. Drezner
Fletcher School of Law and Diplomacy

Dorothy Dwoskin
Microsoft Corporation

Douglas J. Feith
Hudson Institute

Richard H. Fontaine
Center for a New American Security

Aaron L. Friedberg
*Woodrow Wilson School of Public and
International Affairs*

Bonnie S. Glaser
Center for Strategic and International Studies

Susan B. Glasser
Politico

David F. Gordon
International Capital Strategies

Michael J. Green
Center for Strategic and International Studies

Andrew R. Hoehn
RAND Corporation

Kim R. Holmes
Heritage Foundation

Lyndsay C. Howard
International Bank of Azerbaijan

Frederick S. Kempe
Atlantic Council

I. L. Libby
Hudson Institute

James H. Mann
*Johns Hopkins University School of Advanced
International Studies*

Michael A. McDevitt
CNA

47

Council Special Reports

Published by the Council on Foreign Relations

Strategic Stability in the Second Nuclear Age
Gregory D. Koblentz; CSR No. 71, November 2014

U.S. Policy to Counter Nigeria's Boko Haram
John Campbell; CSR No. 70, November 2014
A Center for Preventive Action Report

Limiting Armed Drone Proliferation
Micah Zenko and Sarah Kreps; CSR No. 69, June 2014
A Center for Preventive Action Report

Reorienting U.S. Pakistan Strategy: From Af-Pak to Asia
Daniel S. Markey; CSR No. 68, January 2014

Afghanistan After the Drawdown
Seth G. Jones and Keith Crane; CSR No. 67, November 2013
A Center for Preventive Action Report

The Future of U.S. Special Operations Forces
Linda Robinson; CSR No. 66, April 2013

Reforming U.S. Drone Strike Policies
Micah Zenko; CSR No. 65, January 2013
A Center for Preventive Action Report

Countering Criminal Violence in Central America
Michael Shifter; CSR No. 64, April 2012
A Center for Preventive Action Report

Saudi Arabia in the New Middle East
F. Gregory Gause III; CSR No. 63, December 2011
A Center for Preventive Action Report

Partners in Preventive Action: The United States and International Institutions
Paul B. Stares and Micah Zenko; CSR No. 62, September 2011
A Center for Preventive Action Report

Justice Beyond The Hague: Supporting the Prosecution of International Crimes in National Courts
David A. Kaye; CSR No. 61, June 2011

The Drug War in Mexico: Confronting a Shared Threat
David A. Shirk; CSR No. 60, March 2011
A Center for Preventive Action Report

UN Security Council Enlargement and U.S. Interests
Kara C. McDonald and Stewart M. Patrick; CSR No. 59, December 2010
An International Institutions and Global Governance Program Report

Congress and National Security
Kay King; CSR No. 58, November 2010

Toward Deeper Reductions in U.S. and Russian Nuclear Weapons
Micah Zenko; CSR No. 57, November 2010
A Center for Preventive Action Report

Internet Governance in an Age of Cyber Insecurity
Robert K. Knake; CSR No. 56, September 2010
An International Institutions and Global Governance Program Report

From Rome to Kampala: The U.S. Approach to the 2010 International Criminal Court Review Conference
Vijay Padmanabhan; CSR No. 55, April 2010

Strengthening the Nuclear Nonproliferation Regime
Paul Lettow; CSR No. 54, April 2010
An International Institutions and Global Governance Program Report

The Russian Economic Crisis
Jeffrey Mankoff; CSR No. 53, April 2010

Somalia: A New Approach
Bronwyn E. Bruton; CSR No. 52, March 2010
A Center for Preventive Action Report

The Future of NATO
James M. Goldgeier; CSR No. 51, February 2010
An International Institutions and Global Governance Program Report

The United States in the New Asia
Evan A. Feigenbaum and Robert A. Manning; CSR No. 50, November 2009
An International Institutions and Global Governance Program Report

Intervention to Stop Genocide and Mass Atrocities: International Norms and U.S. Policy
Matthew C. Waxman; CSR No. 49, October 2009
An International Institutions and Global Governance Program Report

Enhancing U.S. Preventive Action
Paul B. Stares and Micah Zenko; CSR No. 48, October 2009
A Center for Preventive Action Report

The Canadian Oil Sands: Energy Security vs. Climate Change
Michael A. Levi; CSR No. 47, May 2009
A Maurice R. Greenberg Center for Geoeconomic Studies Report

The National Interest and the Law of the Sea
Scott G. Borgerson; CSR No. 46, May 2009

Lessons of the Financial Crisis
Benn Steil; CSR No. 45, March 2009
A Maurice R. Greenberg Center for Geoeconomic Studies Report

Global Imbalances and the Financial Crisis
Steven Dunaway; CSR No. 44, March 2009
A Maurice R. Greenberg Center for Geoeconomic Studies Report

Eurasian Energy Security
Jeffrey Mankoff; CSR No. 43, February 2009

Preparing for Sudden Change in North Korea
Paul B. Stares and Joel S. Wit; CSR No. 42, January 2009
A Center for Preventive Action Report

Averting Crisis in Ukraine
Steven Pifer; CSR No. 41, January 2009
A Center for Preventive Action Report

Congo: Securing Peace, Sustaining Progress
Anthony W. Gambino; CSR No. 40, October 2008
A Center for Preventive Action Report

Deterring State Sponsorship of Nuclear Terrorism
Michael A. Levi; CSR No. 39, September 2008

China, Space Weapons, and U.S. Security
Bruce W. MacDonald; CSR No. 38, September 2008

Sovereign Wealth and Sovereign Power: The Strategic Consequences of American Indebtedness
Brad W. Setser; CSR No. 37, September 2008
A Maurice R. Greenberg Center for Geoeconomic Studies Report

Securing Pakistan's Tribal Belt
Daniel S. Markey; CSR No. 36, July 2008 (web-only release) and August 2008
A Center for Preventive Action Report

Avoiding Transfers to Torture
Ashley S. Deeks; CSR No. 35, June 2008

Global FDI Policy: Correcting a Protectionist Drift
David M. Marchick and Matthew J. Slaughter; CSR No. 34, June 2008
A Maurice R. Greenberg Center for Geoeconomic Studies Report

Dealing with Damascus: Seeking a Greater Return on U.S.-Syria Relations
Mona Yacoubian and Scott Lasensky; CSR No. 33, June 2008
A Center for Preventive Action Report

Climate Change and National Security: An Agenda for Action
Joshua W. Busby; CSR No. 32, November 2007
A Maurice R. Greenberg Center for Geoeconomic Studies Report

Planning for Post-Mugabe Zimbabwe
Michelle D. Gavin; CSR No. 31, October 2007
A Center for Preventive Action Report

The Case for Wage Insurance
Robert J. LaLonde; CSR No. 30, September 2007
A Maurice R. Greenberg Center for Geoeconomic Studies Report

Reform of the International Monetary Fund
Peter B. Kenen; CSR No. 29, May 2007
A Maurice R. Greenberg Center for Geoeconomic Studies Report

Nuclear Energy: Balancing Benefits and Risks
Charles D. Ferguson; CSR No. 28, April 2007

Nigeria: Elections and Continuing Challenges
Robert I. Rotberg; CSR No. 27, April 2007
A Center for Preventive Action Report

The Economic Logic of Illegal Immigration
Gordon H. Hanson; CSR No. 26, April 2007
A Maurice R. Greenberg Center for Geoeconomic Studies Report

The United States and the WTO Dispute Settlement System
Robert Z. Lawrence; CSR No. 25, March 2007
A Maurice R. Greenberg Center for Geoeconomic Studies Report

Bolivia on the Brink
Eduardo A. Gamarra; CSR No. 24, February 2007
A Center for Preventive Action Report

After the Surge: The Case for U.S. Military Disengagement From Iraq
Steven N. Simon; CSR No. 23, February 2007

Darfur and Beyond: What Is Needed to Prevent Mass Atrocities
Lee Feinstein; CSR No. 22, January 2007

Avoiding Conflict in the Horn of Africa: U.S. Policy Toward Ethiopia and Eritrea
Terrence Lyons; CSR No. 21, December 2006
A Center for Preventive Action Report

Living with Hugo: U.S. Policy Toward Hugo Chávez's Venezuela
Richard Lapper; CSR No. 20, November 2006
A Center for Preventive Action Report

Reforming U.S. Patent Policy: Getting the Incentives Right
Keith E. Maskus; CSR No. 19, November 2006
A Maurice R. Greenberg Center for Geoeconomic Studies Report

Foreign Investment and National Security: Getting the Balance Right
Alan P. Larson and David M. Marchick; CSR No. 18, July 2006
A Maurice R. Greenberg Center for Geoeconomic Studies Report

Challenges for a Postelection Mexico: Issues for U.S. Policy
Pamela K. Starr; CSR No. 17, June 2006 (web-only release) and November 2006

U.S.-India Nuclear Cooperation: A Strategy for Moving Forward
Michael A. Levi and Charles D. Ferguson; CSR No. 16, June 2006

Generating Momentum for a New Era in U.S.-Turkey Relations
Steven A. Cook and Elizabeth Sherwood-Randall; CSR No. 15, June 2006

Peace in Papua: Widening a Window of Opportunity
Blair A. King; CSR No. 14, March 2006
A Center for Preventive Action Report

Neglected Defense: Mobilizing the Private Sector to Support Homeland Security
Stephen E. Flynn and Daniel B. Prieto; CSR No. 13, March 2006

Afghanistan's Uncertain Transition From Turmoil to Normalcy
Barnett R. Rubin; CSR No. 12, March 2006
A Center for Preventive Action Report

Preventing Catastrophic Nuclear Terrorism
Charles D. Ferguson; CSR No. 11, March 2006

Getting Serious About the Twin Deficits
Menzie D. Chinn; CSR No. 10, September 2005
A Maurice R. Greenberg Center for Geoeconomic Studies Report

Both Sides of the Aisle: A Call for Bipartisan Foreign Policy
Nancy E. Roman; CSR No. 9, September 2005

Forgotten Intervention? What the United States Needs to Do in the Western Balkans
Amelia Branczik and William L. Nash; CSR No. 8, June 2005
A Center for Preventive Action Report

A New Beginning: Strategies for a More Fruitful Dialogue with the Muslim World
Craig Charney and Nicole Yakatan; CSR No. 7, May 2005

Power-Sharing in Iraq
David L. Phillips; CSR No. 6, April 2005
A Center for Preventive Action Report

Giving Meaning to "Never Again": Seeking an Effective Response to the Crisis in Darfur and Beyond
Cheryl O. Igiri and Princeton N. Lyman; CSR No. 5, September 2004

Freedom, Prosperity, and Security: The G8 Partnership with Africa: Sea Island 2004 and Beyond
J. Brian Atwood, Robert S. Browne, and Princeton N. Lyman; CSR No. 4, May 2004

Addressing the HIV/AIDS Pandemic: A U.S. Global AIDS Strategy for the Long Term
Daniel M. Fox and Princeton N. Lyman; CSR No. 3, May 2004
Cosponsored with the Milbank Memorial Fund

Challenges for a Post-Election Philippines
Catharin E. Dalpino; CSR No. 2, May 2004
A Center for Preventive Action Report

Stability, Security, and Sovereignty in the Republic of Georgia
David L. Phillips; CSR No. 1, January 2004
A Center for Preventive Action Report

Note: Council Special Reports are available for download from CFR's website, www.cfr.org.
For more information, email publications@cfr.org.

Made in the USA
Middletown, DE
07 May 2015